A Dress of Locusts

A Dress
of Locusts

SAFA
KHATIB

BLOOMSBURY POETRY
LONDON · OXFORD · NEW YORK · NEW DELHI · SYDNEY

BLOOSMBURY POETRY
Bloomsbury Publishing Plc
50 Bedford Square, London, WC1B 3DP, UK
Bloomsbury Publishing Ireland Limited,
29 Earlsfort Terrace, Dublin 2, D02 AY28, Ireland

BLOOMSBURY, BLOOMSBURY POETRY and the Poetry logo
are trademarks of Bloomsbury Publishing Plc

First published in Great Britain 2025

A catalogue record for this book is available from the British Library

ISBN: PB: : 978-1-5266-6796-0;
eBook: 978-1-5266-6797-7; ePDF: 978-1-5266-6795-3

2 4 6 8 10 9 7 5 3 1

Typeset by Laura Jones-Rivera
Printed and bound in Great Britain by
CPI Group (UK) Ltd, Croydon CR0 4YY

To find out more about our authors and books
visit www.bloomsbury.com and sign up for our newsletters
For product safety related questions contact productsafety@bloomsbury.com

For you who love to endure
thought's chaotic journey—

Contents

LIFE IN MY COUNTRY

Inside the door, past the dread
marquee, there I was,
holding a dark rock, kissing it.
There was someone else
dressed in white cloth, walking
circles around me, chanting.
Sister. Sibling. Stranger. Splendor.

THE DISTANCES

The light was not blue but violet. A voice I remember,
Sumerian, approaching red, raised, resembling
yours. The riding crop against my skin I asked for—
that you come in and welt my lifted thighs. You did.
My clit: the nothing that is.

                                No home. No promise but presence.
You're facing me, holding my hips. This overwhelm
we wander to. Again the pain of what I cannot know
of you penetrates me. A simple scene, not final—
paradise revised, repetitious: this room of grief and pleasure.
And so? What will we risk? I'll go as far as you'll take me,
out of hell, or in. Yes, dear, I'll hold you there.

Myth

The vending machine's bright interior.
I want to climb in. My lips:
the always opening doors. I think
the impossible is sometimes marvelous,
sometimes ghastly. Lately my head
is a Mesoamerican sheath. It's cracked
in places like this card reader,
flashing a red light. It won't work.
I want that. No, that. No, that. Many
things I see poorly or not at all. Some
I see too much. How blunt my thoughts
are, by now. Eisenhower planned
this road. That's true. What I want
I cannot plan. That's the story
of demise. The ancient story of demise.

THE EXECUTIONER

I loved his touch. I touched
myself. I knew from want

his voice would break. He was
in me. I held his fears.

HOTEL

Then I was again
that vacant room. Guests were

various: my death again
and beautiful. Then again,

in different dress. Once,
in a jacquard suit

tapped my goat hoof,
looking out the fogged window—

that's my Janus eye—
watching a crew

replace the backlights
of a billboard. Once,

with hair of snakes,
lips of cold steel, a silica tongue.

Once, in satin sat to smoke
and leaned a plastic ear

against the warming
wall of me. New century.

A closing throat. Not closed.
I love my killed familiars.

DEAR SAFA

you can go

        anywhere you like

  the same image

       follows you

            like a friend

the dead in blue hats

      pulling severed limbs from a black bag

arranging them

        in rows

    over the floor of the white house . . .

*

you can go

        anywhere you like

the conditions of perpetual war

           will comfort you

  they shape

what you may think

and when

*

elsewhere, white phosphorus

coats the night air

and the news

is always the news of your innocence ...

don't worry

about the blacked-out language

of the documents,

the u.s. office of strategic services

translating weltanschauungskrieg

into english in 1941

*

go anywhere you like

even to the islands

of greece

don't worry

when you begin to see agave

kneeling in a camp in lesbos

        cradling the severed head

of her son

        it is all in your head

*

you are one of the good ones

        you have learned well

that the destruction of life

        is a requirement

of national security

        enjoy the expanding canon of english literature

as the u.s. africa command

        conducts torture in the sahel

*

you are one of the good ones

        so go anywhere you like

macron, biden, netanyahu, sunak, scholz

    may appear
        like friends

in your cosmopolitan dream

        in bloodied suits

   singing to the night air: the solution

of the death camp

      we've tried in the levant—

what will come of it?

      what will come of it?

✳

IF NEVER WITH

'Except the face of the divine, everything is vanishing'
says Al-Qasas, the surah of stories. So persistent our fear
of impermanence that we invented the absolute. And how
could I have known that for days now it would be the thought
of your pain, not mine, that excites me. 'I want to go back
and forth between eating you out and caning your palms,'
I text in the morning, the cock cage

                                  you dressed me in
heavy under my jeans. Everyone here is you, you, you.
Hour by hour, 'I' was the need for relation. I made my body
do what I wanted—or I obeyed its demands. Dream was
the engine of intellect. You text: 'Baby, you have a mind
to hurt me, don't you?' I think of your tongue in my muff.
My breasts ache. I reply: 'Let me know when.'

THRESHOLDS

I/ Room of Statues

Entering, curious about the lives

of those idol makers Abraham mocked
you remembered

that here, each all-but-eroded face
could tell you nothing of your life—

You knew your desire was shaped

by that inscrutable obsession
with the forms you learned

your pleasure could assume,
by art—

But you began to feel that what brought you here
was no more remarkable

than what brought you, other times,
to cry in front of mirrors . . .

than what told you you were unable to touch
the origin

of yourself, and yet in love
with quarreling

with what you learned: each line, color, angle

of the face, the body
meant

you looked at what you could.

II/ Earth and Eros

What you called the world,
that mirror you cannot polish—

Once, you believed the self was mirror
you might polish

and in that mirror might see
by whose pure, magisterial will your life unfolds,

but each time you found the mirror is not clean.

Attracted helplessly to invention,
you love to touch the glass—

Among the statues, you wanted something other
than what you saw

in the inexact cruelties and paradoxes of the past

but knew you must, to survive, still honor
and record

the crop's yield, the sun's heat,
the directions of the currents . . .

You must adorn what you see.

III/ What Flourished in Defiance

You left the room of statues, hearing
in the rain,

the makers of idols,
the masters

of the chisel and the rasp—

                *

Walking home, you felt you walked
toward a stand of cedars,

that behind them would lay
the broken

torsos of the gods they carved—

                *

In the Book of Jeremiah: the gods
that did not make

the heavens and the earth
shall perish from the earth

and from under the heavens . . .

Fine, you thought—but what of those
who carved their forms?

You remembered:
the gods are states of mind.

*

At war with the innumerable natures

flourishing within you, knowing,
you too must make

the arc of your life, you understood
nothing

if not that the forgotten dead grow restive—

*

Whether told as tragedy or hard-won triumph,
the idea

of one unimpeachable divine
did not persuade you—

*

You understood
what besieged Abraham

was the fear
that he too was subject

to the unappeasable

need that bid
those makers carve

mere figures, their plain
downcast eyes
                and robes of stone—

                *

Afraid of the unappeasable, he tried
to sate

the will he came to call
Lord, unaccompanied

fog-hidden insect crawling the ground of his mind—

                *

When his father, idol maker,
child

of idol makers, left to the market
Abraham took the hammer—

                *

As when a storm levels, without
any gentler rains of warning, the desert encampments,

leaving the wild cows
to gaze at their calves among the sudden streams

he broke them all, leaving only
the tallest idol,

the hammer slung over its neck—

*

Breaking the idols, Abraham believed
he had conquered

the force of the image—

*

But when the devoted threw him into a pit of flames,
his body,

so like gold, refused to burn—

*

From each conqueror you learned
that to remake the world

you must first invent its past

*

You itched terribly to invent—

*

Walking home on the path, you imagined
Gilgamesh on a street corner in Baghdad,

cupping the U.S. general's ear,

whispering: 'What you call your nation
remains pre-history.

All idols can be broken.'

*

And yet you found the recorders of myth
possessed

by a love for order that does not recognize
a life's sudden

or gradual, unheroic unfurling . . .

*

You found conquered and conqueror, thrown under
that which each claimed to understand—

Thrown under the surface of the revolving
earth . . .

IV/ Epoch

A gasp
      cold and ordinary

curls river-dark beneath the trees—

V/ How Myths Begin

One led the other to a river
where the city ended. They swam, heads
rising with their arms, mid-stroke—
But when, laughing, the one in front
called up, pointing to the crows,
and the other followed, laughing too,
their voices changed, and one felt
the other's body begin to turn, splashing
madly, then found that beloved body
widening into the form of a bull elk,
its head detached, the freed antlers clashing
among the stones that tossed in the currents.
By the legs one pulled the mass of the other
who had become a stranger, unable now
to respond, one whose unmoored head, drifting
away, stared back across the growing
distance, the large eyes shyly blinking.
But reaching land, one looked down
at the other, tossing, tangled in the weeds,
and found a human body, whole, attempting to speak.

*

There was no gentleness, in the digging.
Lifting a wet, fragmented rock
the living cut through the soft dirt,
then, dissatisfied, turned to discard it
into pile, and walked, searching for a clean rock
at the water's edge, and returned
to dig again. This was how the nights proceeded,

but the wind would not relent, and the stones fell
and fell from that unholy makeshift cairn, the dirt
blowing back into the long depression
that despite those hours of digging never
deepened enough to hold the form that waited
there, beside it, the head turned toward the river.

VI/ Unmastered, the Earth Turns

Then the style of night
was to admit everything—

the deaths you watched
the deaths you ignored

in the nights of that veiled world

your learned song
your wanting mind

VII/ Elegy

The beloved has not deceived you.
Nobody vanished, shape-shifting, faithless into the dark—

Look up at the city: the immaculate record, the mere history
of the simple terrors by which you lived.

APOLOGY

After he had folded his sketch
and tucked it into the box
labeled 'letters' but which
contained, in fact,
only the others he sometimes
drew in our separations and
which I only saw when he
returned, or when I opened,
after nights of anger,
the door again—a human
with the head of a jay, a tiger
with a crow's wings—I watched
him, as I spoke, begin another.

As for What's Left

The imam, in those days, owned three animals:
one winged, one beaked but wingless now, for injury,
one hooved—or that's how he explained them
as we rested, half-clothed, in front of the mihrab
long after the other worshippers had left. The smell
of their bodies still lingered in the carpets,
so that as he entered me, it was difficult
to feel we were alone, exactly, or that there was
much difference, in the end, between the undisciplined
motion of fucking and the more predictable motion
of those who come daily to bow to you, Lord. Once,
I described you to another, whose singing voice
I've nearly forgotten by now, as a fog-hidden insect
crawling the ground of the mind . . . That doesn't
seem true anymore. I would pray with the others.
But after, I would wait for all to leave but the one
who led the prayer, the one in whom I thought I saw
what you deny me, as if sex were where the distinctions
I'd for so long been taught—between reason
and ecstasy, duty and joy—might, as I reached
back for him, lose their power . . . That's how
naïve I was. Nothing really changed. After each night,
I'd drive home to my neighbor, who would weep
simply, openly, as I rubbed his neuropathic feet.
Yet it is true that what I once called my sorrow-
unto-death—a dark lake in which there is only to drift
until lost for good—I began, in the mosque, to see
more clearly as mere sorrow, as the color I'd assigned
to the lake, with which the lake had nothing to do.

In the Remains of the Mosque

Beside the fallen minarets, beneath which
rest the remains of the shrine
to Dionysus—the mosaic of his thrown-back head

surrounded by dancing animals—
beneath which rests the rock
bearing the trace of the Aramean verse
that, even now, makes way

for the water flowing against it—
the water that runs beneath what can be seen—
two snakes entwine their copper bodies in the dirt.

DEAR SAFA

Your gestures of devotion before the one
you longed to taste, to let enter you
each time in a different bed, by a different name:
Fashioner, Conqueror, Nourisher, Judge—

Remember them now—

You have for so long exalted the mind,
but you were once a rough surface
in a kind of light you cannot remember.

Water spilled over your hands.
Strangers gathered about you and took rest.

✳

AT MARY'S

Dream pop, oak walls, a ceiling lined with steampunk flowers.
I'm beside you, watching bad porn on the TV above the bar.
There are other lives I might have lived. Sometimes anatomy
is a ruse, a spectacular impatience. I'm in love with that green thong.
Nature is possibility. Under certain conditions, an idea can penetrate.
The actors cum. I remember Amina calling me from Bangladesh:
'I have the hormones, but you must take care of me. Tell me what to do.'
I think the lure of autonomy terrifies us.

                                   You're in love with Josephine,
the name you've given to perpetual disappointment. My mother often said
'you must be careful with impulses.' She was in love with the neutral.
The night she died I awoke in the kitchen to the open door of the microwave.
The eye of science. Nostalgia is instructive. The maddening
traces of some suffering inhabit the mind like melody.

Then the assembly dispersed to the ships,

     the soldiers craving food and sleep—

but Akheel stayed back . . .

*

Ahora el desvelo domina
el sueño que domina el dolor . . .

*

He mourned over Patroklos, remembering his nerve

     and how many battles bihi juhdan ma'an

and how many sea swells nālahuma al-juhd

*

He turned onto his left side, then again upon his face
y el dolor aumentó

*

Se levantó.
   Multa'an.
     Lágrimas, lágrimas . . .

As one who's lost his mind roams the harsh shore
he wandered until by light of dawn

sea and land grew bright—

*

Then he yoked his horse to the chariot,
and to the back of the chariot

                    he tied Hector

and rode, dragging him around the pyre
three times

          then returned exhausted to the tents

y le abandonó

                    face-down, sprawled out en al-tarab—

Instances of Ishtar

I

I am racked
              by memories

     of the goddess—

In one, she hands me
a dress
       of locusts. It gleams

a red gaze. I put it on.
It seems

my body hums,
a gathering
         of long muted voices.

I walk with her

through the cedar forest
which opens
         onto a shoreline

covered in wires
and weapons
       and bulbs—
the waste
          of cities.

We stare into the waves—

II

In another memory,
I am standing over dark water

where a stranger is
greedily drinking.

Turning toward me, the stranger cries

    lama sabachthani

        Why have you

    forsaken me

The corrupted
             cry of Christ, but godless—

I sift through the sand.
The faceless doll washes up

in my hands, my mind
a grey storm,
          the bell

of me, soundless—

She is always at a distance,
turning back—

III

Sometimes the sea was
the border
                   between freedom

and lament—
                   I lived centuries

in transit. I heard
Al-Khansā, Cassandra,

the disenchanted prophets, women

of Greece
                   and Palestine and Iraq—

We walked the coast in fits of laughter
and mourning
                   toward

Helen who sat on a bed
of driftwood
                   weaving

jeweled garments:
                   anecdota

      tawarīkh

records of the days, the days—

      my soul:
                   a shutter
which opens
                   and opens . . .

JAHILIYYAS

I

Walking to the city of Lixus
on the African coast, I neared
a gaunt cow in the morning fog.

At a distance, its head seemed
a vessel draped in torn cloth.
I imagined it held up by Al-Khansa

in exile, as if it were a kind of prism
through which the light of kinship
might still come, after the years of lament.

Then the neck of the animal, its hair
raised in the cold wind, then the body
twisted into view. I walked closer.

Black oil spilled from its eyes. I heard
faint weeping, faint laughter elsewhere.
The animal turned and sniffed the ground.

A dark pool gathered around us.
I looked in. I touched my neck.
I became a lift of starlings in the gleaming hour.

II

Each evening, the muezzin
                              at my door

                                                    He knew not to sing

    any verse from the Book
                              The television on the far wall

On the kitchen floor I listened
                              to his call

In recitation

                    the higher registers
                                        are forbidden

Like that
                    A broadcast
                                        'The Asian Century'

'Projected Economic Growth . . .'

                                        in Maharashtra, over five thousand

    farmer suicides
                              'I enjoyed you'

he said, in love

                    with the idea

of eternal property, eternal comfort,

the pearls of heaven

                        He was a muezzin
        I wanted

                                to release him

from the idea
                The pearls of heaven

        melting on his stomach

                        His voice in the higher registers

tall shadow on the far wall
                                as if an angel

                Al-Qāri'ah
                        What could make you understand

Al-Qāri'ah . . .
                O catastrophe,
                                my origin

39

III

For ten nights the goats wailed on the roof.

They pulled at the ropes
which bound them to the cistern.

Nobody would come to sacrifice them.

He carried the parts of the broken statue
into the bedroom
of the house he'd inherited.

He left and entered, left and entered.

A small tower rose in front of the mirror
in which he'd once watched me undress.

I lay beneath the window, listening to his movements,

dreaming of his exhausted mouth,
draped in the knowledge of his dead.

I am only the nightly visitor.

THOSE HOURS

I could say that my pleasure, beneath him,
was a meadow, dark in places, brighter
in others, and that at the farthest edge
there grew pleasure's
                          more unruly varieties—
Rapture. Terror. But the plain
truth is that his touch first meant
my power, then his, then mine again,
then, soon enough, if not kindness,
                          the illusion of kindness,
illusion that, for some time, had been enough.
Where I lie down tonight there is no field,
no other. There are the windows of this room
and the windows,
                          elsewhere, of other rooms.

DEAR SAFA

Beneath what you wish to lament
lies what you have not learned to lament—

halls of the past that still bewilder you . . .

Passing the half-built high-rise
the piles of dirt
                the gleaming tools

look in long enough

to notice beside the briefly abandoned cranes
the Lady of Warka

lifting a purple heart from the dirt, brushing it clean—

The violence you know
is not the act of the stranger—

It is your sustenance: this continent
which remains

the American night, the ancestral crime—

See that your face
is so like her alabaster face:

record of a past, altered beyond recognition.

✻

ABSENCE IS THE GUIDE

When I found my wound would not clot
I cut two even strips of the day's newspaper
and pressed them

                into the cut's by-now-uncertain
depth and held a lighter close enough
that the flame might touch,
the paper's edge—

                but hearing the steps of others
walking near, I turned to watch
two strangers who,

                as I prepared to speak,
turned away, then crouched
to photograph the cypress knees
at the pond's edge

                as slowly, first
with relief, then the familiar
nausea of an unnamable awe, I knew
I had forgotten

                the face of who or what it was
that pierced me here, or when—

ELEGIACS

I

tethered to what in the dark I   found at the edge of the grasses

still as a bowl full of water   skull of a fox in the cold

crack in the wintering jawbone   flowering no-place of eyelids

who with a rope in my youth   tied to my wrist this once-head?

dry in the throats of the hunters   still in the distance the voices

come so like friends from the far   grasses I cannot now see

II

what of myself could I sing now   bound to this death of another

move and it moves, but when still   slow in my shadow it leaks

storming the mind's stark harbor   bright the idea then it harshens

sea-less midwestern this soft   ground where an asylum once stood

burials burials unholy   rites in the making of nations

land where I've made my one life   bound to this vessel, I walk

III

windows where guests stood watching   bodies of patients in the darkening

land was once lake was once ocean   brow of the moon god glistening

IV

plain of the terrible presence here where the enemy fell

stripped of their gleaming armor piles of their bronze in the dirt

here where we'd named ourselves victor seeds in such ruthless beginning

ice in the eyes of gazelles hymn-heavied tongue in the dew

V

days of inviolate mourning   open to other exteriors

hawks in the half-light, the hunt   touch and be touched in the gold

AMONG ASPHODELS

Someone sleeps in fits
before a screen on which,
in the final scene, the detective
mutters his epiphany . . .

Stranger, what would I say to you
who will not have known me,
who minutes after my death will drink
a glass of water in a far room.

SILHOUETTE

The almost imperceptible
breathing
            of the iridescent

creature floating across the tank—

The ceiling leaks.
Small drops fall into the water.

Standing in the doorway, looking in,
I do not hear
my body, my breath—

The intruder has come and gone.

ONE SHORE, THEN ANOTHER

Now thought assumes the color of time with you:
an interruption in the florid darks of the city—
sudden, sourceless. Someone walking by in the street
keeps saying 'come here' to someone out of view.
I can hear them run toward each other or away.
You're in the other room, painting. My eye can't choose
between the surfaces of this one.
                         I want to walk in
and tell you something about those Spanish horses
alone on an island in the Carolinas. A shipwreck in 1580,
then centuries of wild horses. Bewilderment, then despair,
then wonder—that isn't their story. They are not
the horses of Achilles. They do not weep for us . . .

Acknowledgements

The following poems have appeared in journals and magazines, sometimes in other versions:

'Hotel' and 'Those Hours' in *The Kenyon Review*

'The Distances,' 'If Never With,' 'At Mary's' and 'One Shore, Then Another' in *manywor(l)ds*

A Note on the Author

Safa Khatib is a poet, translator, teacher and daughter of South Indian immigrants. Her writing has appeared in numerous journals, including *Words Without Borders*, the *Baffler*, the *Kenyon Review* and the *White Review*. She is the recipient of support from the US Fulbright Program and the Stadler Center for Poetry, among other institutions. She is currently a PhD student in the Track for International Writers in the department of Comparative Literature at Washington University in St Louis, Missouri.

A Note on the Type

Warnock is a serif typeface designed by Robert Slimbach. The design features sharp, wedge-shaped serifs. The typeface is named after John Warnock, one of the co-founders of Adobe. John Warnock's son, Chris Warnock, requested that Slimbach design the typeface as a tribute to his father in 1997. It was later released as a commercial font by Adobe in 2000 under the name Warnock Pro.

If you enjoyed *A Dress of Locusts*, you might like
I cannot be good until you say it by Sanah Ahsan:

PASSPORT

Veiled by tablecloth, my girlfriend swats
my hand, a fly on her knee. The teaspoons
are touching in public. Her grandmother
offers me a salami stick to start. *Sorry I
don't eat pork.* Grandmother's voice rises a
plastic octave, *sorry I don't understand why
muslims do that.* Her wrinkled grip drops
the pepperoni-packed ramekin back down
at the table's epicentre. I say: *pigs eat their
own shit!* My laugh meets an active silence
and two half-smiles. I am one among six
white faces. I check my phone under the
table: yep no one has messaged since two
minutes ago. *Sorry, so you're a psychologist?*
I nod, ignoring Grandmother's butchering
of my name, swine remnants poking
from her incisors. A bamboo bowl brims
with plum tomatoes, dewy rocket, purple
cabbage, اَلـرَّزَاقُ and sun-pepper saviours.
I reach for relief in the rainbow when her
grandmother asks *do you have a British
passport?* The burgundy-red stamped with
a golden crest moves more than my limp
tongue. I muster up the lion's courage to ask
are we going somewhere?